Paul Revere

American Freedom Fighter

by Wil Mara

Content Consultant

Nanci R. Vargus, Ed.D.
Professor Emeritus, University of Indianapolis

Reading Consultant

Jeanne M. Clidas, Ph.D.
Reading Specialist

Children's Press®
An Imprint of Scholastic Inc.

Library of Congress Cataloging-in-Publication Data
Mara, Wil.
  Paul Revere / by Wil Mara ; poem by Jodie Shepherd.
    pages cm. -- (Rookie biographies)
  Includes index.
  ISBN 978-0-531-21411-4 (library binding) -- ISBN 978-0-531-20597-6 (pbk.)
  1. Revere, Paul, 1735-1818--Juvenile literature. 2. Statesmen--Massachusetts--
Biography--Juvenile literature. 3. Massachusetts--Biography--Juvenile literature.
4. Massachusetts--History--Revolution, 1775-1783--Juvenile literature. I. Shepherd,
Jodie. II. Title.

  F69.R43M275 2015
  973.3'311092--dc23
  [B]   2015017320

Produced by Spooky Cheetah Press
Poem by Jodie Shepherd
Design by Keith Plechaty

Printed in China 62

SCHOLASTIC, CHILDREN'S PRESS, ROOKIE BIOGRAPHIES®, and associated logos
are trademarks and/or registered trademarks of Scholastic Inc.

1 2 3 4 5 6 7 8 9 10 R 25 24 23 22 21 20 19 18 17 16

Photographs ©: cover: GraphicaArtis/Corbis Images; 3 top left: Don Troiani/
Corbis Images; 3 top right: Don Troiani/Corbis Images; 3 bottom: Jorge Salcedo/
Shutterstock, Inc.; 4: GL Archive/Alamy Images; 8: Marcio Jose Bastos Silva/
Shutterstock, Inc.; 11: Ivy Close Images/Alamy Images; 12, 15 top: North Wind Picture
Archives; 15 bottom, 19: Peter Newark American Pictures/Bridgeman Art Library;
20: Collection of the New-York Historical Society, USA/Bridgeman Art Library;
23: National Army Museum, London/Bridgeman Art Library; 24: Courtesy of The
Bostonian Society; 27: DustyDingo/Alamy Images; 28: Superstock, Inc.; 30 top
left, 30 top right: Peter Newark American Pictures/Bridgeman Art Library; 31 top:
Collection of the New-York Historical Society, USA/Bridgeman Art Library; 31 center:
Superstock, Inc.; 31 bottom: Bettmann/Corbis Images.

Table of Contents

Meet Paul Revere

Today, if there is an emergency, we can pick up a phone. We call for help fast. That was not the case when Paul Revere was alive. Messages were passed through letters, or when one person spoke to another.

One night in 1775, Revere had to spread one of the most important messages in American history.

Paul Revere was born in Boston, Massachusetts, on December 21, 1734. At this time, there was no United States. America was an English **colony**. It was ruled by the King of England.

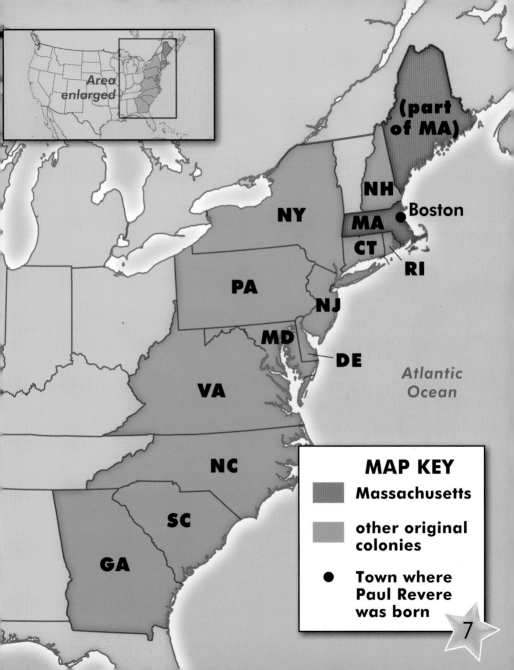

Area enlarged

(part of MA)

NH

• Boston

NY

MA

CT

RI

PA

NJ

MD

DE

VA

Atlantic Ocean

NC

SC

GA

MAP KEY

Massachusetts

other original colonies

• Town where Paul Revere was born

More than 250 years later, Revere's home still stands in Boston.

Revere's father was a **silversmith**. He made objects, such as dishes and cups, out of silver. When Paul was a teenager, he learned his father's craft. After his father died in 1754, Revere took over the family business. Three years later, he married Sarah Orne. They had eight children.

Freedom Fighter

By the early 1770s, many Americans wanted to be free of England. They did not want to be ruled by the King anymore. Revere was one of those people. They were called **Patriots**.

The King of England sent soldiers to America. They were there to keep the Patriots under control.

English soldiers wore red jackets. That is why they were sometimes called "Redcoats."

There were no cars back then. But a messenger on horseback could spread news quickly.

In 1773, Revere's wife died. Later, he married Rachel Walker. They also had eight children.

This was the year that Revere became a messenger. He rode a horse to nearby cities. He told people there what the English soldiers were doing. This information helped Patriots get ready. They knew they might have to defend themselves against English soldiers.

The Midnight Ride

On April 18, 1775, Revere took the ride that would make him famous. English soldiers were planning to capture two Patriot leaders: John Hancock and Samuel Adams.

FAST FACT!

In 1776, Hancock and Adams both signed the Declaration of Independence. This was a letter to the King of England. It let him know why the colonies would fight to be free.

John
Hancock

Samuel
Adams

15

Paul Revere's Midnight Ride

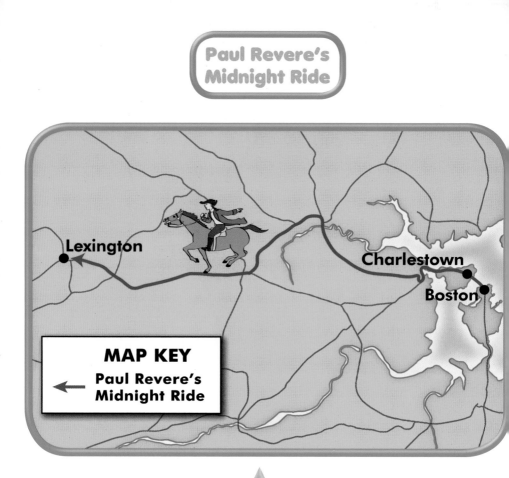

Lexington

Charlestown

Boston

MAP KEY

← Paul Revere's Midnight Ride

Revere was captured by English soldiers as he rode out of Lexington. He was later released.

Revere rode to the town of Charlestown. He woke people up to warn them that English soldiers were coming.

He continued on to Lexington, waking as many people as he could along the way. When he arrived in town, Revere met up with Hancock and Adams. Thanks to his warning, they were able to get away safely.

Everyone thinks Revere yelled, "The British are coming! The British are coming!" as he rode. He actually said, "The Regulars are coming out!" Regulars is what English soldiers were called.

FAST FACT!

Revere became famous thanks to a poem called "Paul Revere's Ride." It was written by an American poet named Henry Wadsworth Longfellow.

19

This is a photo of paper money that Paul Revere helped to create.

Doing His Part

The next day, war broke out between England and the American colonies. Revere wanted to help in any way that he could.

The colonists wanted to have their own country. They needed their own money. Revere used his **engraving** skills to make some of the first American money.

The American soldiers needed powder to fire their guns. But they did not have enough. Revere figured out how to make a lot of gunpowder at once. He set up a factory. Now gunpowder could be made day and night.

In 1776, Revere joined a militia (muh-LISH-uh) in Boston. A militia is a group of people who are not in the army but who take part in the fighting during a war.

A Boston militia fighting English soldiers

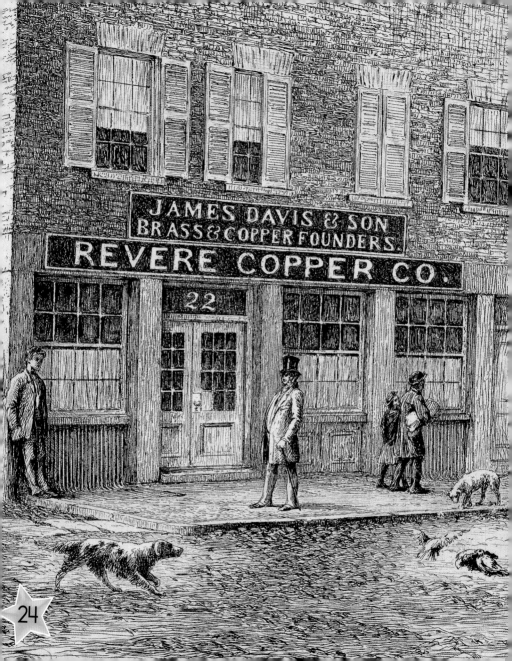

The American Revolutionary War ended in April 1783. The colonists were free from England. They called their new country the United States of America.

Revere went back to his silversmithing business. He began working with other metals, too. These included iron, bronze, and copper.

This illustration shows Paul Revere's Copper Company.

This bell, made by Revere, is on display in Massachusetts.

Products made of metal were very expensive. Only rich people could afford them. Revere found a way to make metal objects more cheaply. Now more people could afford nice things.

FAST FACT!

Many of Paul Revere's handmade products still exist. People collect them!

27

Timeline of Paul Revere's Life

1775
makes his famous ride

1734
born on December 21

Paul Revere died on May 10, 1818, at his home in Boston. He was 83 years old. Revere will always be best remembered for his midnight ride. But he did much to help America become a free country. He also proved that one person can truly make a world of difference.

1818
dies on May 10

1801
starts the Revere Copper Company

A Poem About Paul Revere

Because he wanted to be free,

Paul took a ride for liberty.

He warned that the British were coming to fight—

and galloped into history that night.

You Can Make a Difference

- Do not be afraid to stand up for what you feel is right, even if others do not agree with you.

- Do not be afraid to try out new ideas.

- Believe that *you* can make a difference.

Glossary

colony (KOHL-uh-nee): territory that has been settled by people from another country and is controlled by that country

engraving (en-GRAYV-ing): cutting words or designs onto a hard surface

Patriots (PAY-tree-uhts): colonists living in America before the Revolutionary War who fought to be free of England's rule

silversmith (SIL-vur-smith) someone who makes things out of silver

Index

Facts for Now

Visit this Scholastic Web site for more information on Paul Revere:
www.factsfornow.scholastic.com
Enter the keywords **Paul Revere**

About the Author

Wil Mara is the award-winning author of more than 140 books, many of which are educational titles for children.

J B REVERE

Mara, Wil.
Paul Revere

SOF

R4002319918

SOUTH FULTON BRANCH
Atlanta-Fulton Public Library